THE MOONLIT REVERIES

A SOLILOQUY TO THE STARS

MS SONAM KUMAR

Made with ❤ on the BookLeaf Publishing Platform

www.bookleafpub.in

www.bookleafpub.com

Dedication

It is rightly said that "Life is like a river flowing ceaselessly, carrying with it the serenity of stillness and the promise of continuity." I have long nurtured the dream of authoring a book, awaiting that defining moment of inspiration to pour my thoughts onto paper. The list of those to whom I owe my gratitude is endless, but at its very forefront stand my parents Shri Vijay Kumar and Late Smt Rajeshwari, the pillars of my existence.

My father and mother have been the wind beneath my wings, breathing life into my aspirations and depth into my ideas. I have always believed that while one can never truly repay their parents, the greatest tribute is to make them proud.

Every soul who has woven warmth and meaning into my life has left an imprint on these pages. My beloved husband, Mr Mohit Pawar, has been my greatest strength, my guiding star and unshakeable pillar. His quiet resolve steadies me in moments of doubt, and his mountain belief in me has been the driving force behind my journey. In my triumphs, his pride shines brighter than my own, and in my struggles, his presence becomes my greatest comfort. He has walked beside me not just in moments of joy, but through every trial, reminding me that love is not only about sharing smiles but also about standing strong through storms.

My dearest sister, Ms Monika, has been a constant source of strength through every storm and sunshine. Her quiet resilience and boundless love have given me the courage to rise even when the path seemed uncertain. In her laughter, I have found joy, and in her wisdom, I have found peace. My esteemed brother-in-law, Mr Abhijeet, has been a steady presence, his quiet strength guiding me like a silent compass.

My heartfelt gratitude extends to my gracious mother-in-law, Smt. Pushpa Pawar, whose wisdom brings calmness to my heart and whose presence feels like a quiet blessing. Her gentle words have been a source of comfort, and her grace has taught me the beauty of patience and strength. My respected father-in-law, Dr M.P. Singh, has been a guiding light, his strength inspiring me to face life with resilience. His wisdom has quietly shaped my thoughts, reminding me that true success lies not only in achievements but in the values we uphold.

My kind-hearted sister-in-law, Ms Mansi, turns simple moments into treasured memories with her warmth and sincerity. Her thoughtful nature and endless kindness have made every gathering a little brighter.

My ever-supportive brother-in-law, Mr Rajdeep Shekhawat, strengthens my journey with his steady *presence - a quiet reassurance that no matter the path, family is always near. The heart of our home, our beloved Sasha, fills our world with innocence and laughter - a sweet reminder that life's purest joys are found in the simplest moments.*

My beloved brothers, Mr Praveen Kumar and Mr Amit Kumar, have been the foundation of my strength always standing by me with quiet yet powerful support. My cherished sisters-in-law, Ms Sonia Kumar and Ms. Jyoti, have brought warmth and affection into my life, adding comfort to every corner of my heart. The little stars of my universe- Pritesh, Myra, Nyra, Granth, Divisha, Prithvi, and Abhiraj, sprinkle my world with joy, their innocent laughter filling my heart with light.

The blessings of my revered uncle and aunt Late Shri Santaram and Smt Panmeshwari, echo through my life like a timeless opus, reminding me that love trespasses time.

My brothers, Mr Ashok, Mr Mahesh, Mr Abhey, and Mr Dev, have been silent pillars of strength, while my dear sisters-in-law, Ms Kavita, Ms Rajeshwari, Ms Savita, and Ms Anjali, have filled my life with their quiet support and warmth. My treasured nieces and nephews- Vaishnavi, Radhika, Shivam, Vanshika, Satyam, Diksha, Sundaram, and Riddhi- light my path with their vibrant energy and love.

To Vishal Bhaiya, Amit Bhaiya, Nidhi Bhabhi, Pupu, Rohit Bhaiya, Rishi Bhaiya, and Sumit Bhaiya-your collective wisdom and steadfast encouragement have been the silent pillars underpinning this endeavor. A special mention to the entire Franciscan team, whose resolute support and guidance have been a source of strength. Your belief in me has illuminated my path, reminding me that success is always sweeter when shared with those who truly believe in you.I am deeply grateful to my dearest friends and hear sisters, Neha Ahmad, Nikita Kasana, and Kadiyam Arpitha, who have been my constants through every season of life. My soul brothers, Atif and Gaurav, have been more than friends, they have been my anchors, reminding me that family is not always defined by blood, but by the people who stand by you without question. Whatever I am today, I owe to the love and guidance of my friends, especially Neha, whose presence has been my greatest gift. Her endless faith in me has carried me through my darkest moments, and her kindness has been the gentle push I needed to rise again.

My little bundles of joy, Rabah and Vaidehi, are the sweetest melody of my heart, their laughter reminds me that joy is found in the simplest of things. My dearest little sisters, Nisha, Arisha, and Alisha, your love and innocence have filled my world with endless warmth and comfort, reminding me that even in life's most difficult moments, family is the greatest strength of all.

Every page of this book is a tribute to those who have stood by me, through my victories and my struggles. To each of you who has walked this journey with me, your love is the quiet strength behind every word written here, and the light that continues to guide me forward.

Preface

In the stillness of midnight, when the world takes a siesta and silence weaves its own melodies, the soul finds its truest voice. It is in these pristine moments of solitude that emotions unfurl like petals kissed by moonlight, and thoughts, unconstrained, dance in the company of stars. 'The Moonlit Reveries - A Soliloquy to the Stars' is not merely a collection of poems; it is a saga through the avenues of human emotion, where love whispers through the swishing leaves, nostalgia lingers like an autumn breeze, and hope shines like a outlying constellation.

Each poem in this book is an ode to the unspoken, a tribute to the delicate tremors of the heart that often go unnoticed in the sunshine of the day. Poetry captures the depth of human emotions, from gentle longing to bold dreams, from past sorrows to the bright light of resilience. Each poem reflects the heart's journey, knitted with dreams, hope, and the endless search for meaning under the vast sky.

The moon, with its mystical glow, listens intently to the murmurs of poets, lovers, and wanderers alike. The stars, twinkling with ageless wisdom, bear witness to the silent confessions of weary souls. And this book, dear readers, is an invitation to sit beneath the vastness of the night sky, let the words seep into your spirit, and find solace in the gentle clasp of poetry.

In 2008, my mother ascended to the heavens, becoming the moon itself a celestial guardian who now bathes my path in her ethereal glow. It is in this luminous reflection that the title of my work finds its essence.

Acknowledgements

My soul overflows, a silent offering to the vast, starlit canvas that birthed *'The Moonlit Reveries - A Soliloquy to the Stars.'* This collection, a whisper of dreams, would have remained locked within the chambers of my heart, had not the radiant spirits I now address illuminated my path.

To Ms <u>Yashika Bhardwaj</u>, my first Principal leader who helped me as a guiding star, my mentor: your wisdom, a divine insignia, has directed me through the darkest nights of doubt. Your belief, a gentle hand upon my trembling spirit, has sculpted not only this work, but the very essence of my creative being.

I extend my heartfelt gratitude to my esteemed Principal, <u>Ms Seema Behl</u>, for her constant support and encouragement. Your belief in me has given me the strength to pursue my creative vision with confidence and clarity. Your leadership has been a guiding light, inspiring me to grow both professionally and personally.

My sincere thanks to my revered Principal <u>Dr Sarita Pande</u> for her insightful guidance faith in my abilities. Your wisdom has shaped my path, and your encouragement has given me the courage to stay true to my creative journey.

To my cherished sisters, Ms Sapna Ahuja, Ms Ginni Sharma, Ms Ria Sekhri, Ms Vasudha, Ms Vinita, Ms Neha Mishra and Ms. Nidhi , you are my safe place, my guiding stars. Your love has been a warm hug in the cold moments of doubt, giving me strength when I needed it most. You've cheered for every small win, every quiet word, with a joy that filled the silence. Your faith, steady and quiet, has helped me through sleepless nights and restless days.

To each of you, my guiding lights your presence is a comfort, your words a calm, your love a bond that can't be broken. This work, filled with hope and gratitude, belongs to you as much as it does to me.

1. The Chained Soul

Prison is a home where you live like a tenant,
Where one swings like a thread in the air.
Somewhere attached and somewhere detached,

The Sun gazes through the iron bars
Where heart longs for the nearest star
The silent footsteps echo an opus of stillness,
Perfectly entwined with the soul's lone illness.

Time moves slow, like a fading trace,
Memories blur in this silent space.
Laughter is rare, shadows grow tall,
And each day feels like an endless fall.

Yet hope still flickers, faint but bright,
A whispering voice in the quiet night.
For even a caged bird hums its song,
Knowing it won't be trapped for long.

2. The Hands That Held Me

My mother, a beautiful angel,
Descended on a barren land
And spread her wings on the golden sand.

Flowers blossomed when she walked the path,
Her smile faded all the gloomy clouds.
A presence so pristine, a heart so bright,
She lifted my sorrows and her love was the only hope
that I could borrow.

My mother, a metaphor of happiness and light,
Got separated from me.
Making my life dry and torn,
Like a lone and withered tree standing amid a
thunderstorm.

I talk to her under the moonlight,
And tears are shed in the shadows of grey night.
She listens to my heartbeat's fall,
Through whispers in the silvered light.

And all my problems are taken to her by the stars.

She is the opus of my soaring heights.
A ray of hope, my sunshine dear,
Guiding me through endless nights.

She is a colourful butterfly,
That flies in the darkened sky.
At the end, opening my heart,
She gave me wisdom none deny.

But didn't teach me how to survive,
Without her love to hold.
In 2008, my world turned dark,
Yet I walked on, brave and bold.
And sometimes, it's hard as stone to stay strong,
Especially for a motherless child when things go wrong.

(Dedicated to my mother, Late Smt Rajeshwari)

3. Moonlit Shadows: In the Lap of My Father's Love

And if you ask me what keeps me going after my
mother's death,
My answer will always be my dad, my guiding breath.

He silently became my shadow without uttering a word,
And I vibrantly became his reflection, our bond
undeterred.
He is my moonlight amid the glimmering black clouds,
And my only hope in doubt, when uncertainty
enshrouds.

Just as God is invisible, so are my dad's blessings,
His charisma and charm, my heart's true confessing.
He makes me face the thunderstorm with pristine calm,

I always say one can never repay their parents,
but make them proud, our lifelong psalm.
Through every trial and joy that life imparts,
His love remains the compass of our hearts.

(Dedicated to my father, Shri Vijay Kumar)

4. The Ever-Turning Pages of Seasons

With the flip of every page,
The colour of every season changes.
From twilight to greyness,
The night always rearranges.

Spring blossoms like a heart of a lover,
Autumn loses hope, like the sun in winter's cover.
Summer brings light to the heart of many,
And winter covers spaces with flakes so snowy.

Monsoon brings the joys of life,
In the form of rain, washing away all strife.
Where plants bloom just like a seedling's rise,
Reaching for the sky, bathed in golden height.

5. Seeds of Betrayal

Once upon a time,
The seeds of kindness and sacrifice were sown,
They struggled to bloom, yet were left alone,
As the soil of selfishness turned them to stone.

Just like this
Someone's life became a metaphor
Roaring the silent sighs of the pain
From a connection, once pure, now torn,
As fragile threads cavill in the rain.

Your own people will tear your soul apart,
Then they will play that whatever is happening
With you is God's Art.

They'll bind your heart with gilded lies,
Sculpting your spirit beneath their eyes,
Claiming the agony, the ache, the scars,
Are part of a masterpiece painted in the stars.

But behind the oaks, your truth will fade,
Lost in the shadows of what they have portrayed,
And you'll wander, fractured, without a voice,
Wondering if you had ever really had a choice.

6. Wings of Hope and Love

Breaking the shackles and chains of pain,
A river of kindness flows through the strain.
People like pebbles stand adrift,
Caught in the overflow's endless shift.

Life is flexible, a beautiful art,
Just like you, a song in my heart.
My heart, deep as the river's depth
Keeps sensing the ache all along.

An inner voice pulled me down in despair,
But you held my hand and you were there.
The blue river shone like glitter in your eyes,
Giving wings to my revery, letting me rise.

You are the Soliloquy
and the Tiffany of my life.
(Dedicated to revered husband Mohit Ji)

7. The Silent Storms and Unheard Struggles of Men

The Story of Men Behind the Stoic Mask
Beneath stoic exteriors, silent storms brew,
Bearing unseen burdens, their strength misconstrued.

Men,
Men, the ones who fight every battle silently,
The doors open for them to expectations daily.

Their voices become voiceless as avenues unfold,
And they become subjected to tensions untold.
The lens through which society views them,
Should be diminished with the bonds between men.

It's time to talk about their mental silence,
Which can only be broken by changing the ongoing
violence
Against the set defiance.
Let's break the chains of silent compliance,
Together, we stand against the quiet violence.

8. A Heart Sealed in Silence

Flipping the pages, turn by turn,
Stirs the mind with the thoughts unseen
Hoping every line will create a rhyme in the scene
A storm of whispers dances beneath the skin,
Revealing truths that lie within.

An over-thinker speaks to the moon,
While shadows murmur a haunting tune.
His mind, a river wild and deep,
Where jagged stones cut through his sleep.

Hope glimmers like stars at dawn,
Yet fears rise swift when light is gone.
He climbs the staircase of fragile light,
Seeking peace beneath the veil of night.

A hero at sunrise, villain by eve,
Truth and illusion make him grieve.
Thoughts bloom like rain upon the shore,
Yet drown in silence evermore.

Caught between sky and restless stream,
An over-thinker lives in a dream.
Rooted like trees, swayed by the breeze,
Lost in the mirage of unseen seas.

9. Somewhere between Truth and Lies

Truth sifts through the sieve of words,
Slipping like sand through quivering hands.
A soft murmur, easily broken by a harsh word.
It stands intricate, balanced on thin air,

Crushing under the weight of doubt.
A quiet flare in the dark,
Lost when shadows stretch too far like the sand dunes.
It bends beneath fear and silent moons.

And crumbles when trust dims.
Yet, in its rawest form,
Truth remains brittle yet critical.

10. Silent Murmurs of the Sunset

The pale twilight that dances on the dusk of colours,
Breathes life into the lifeless, soft as the moon's lover.
It births a phoenix from the ashes bright,
Fire and light tangled in the arms of night.

A person views the sky with stars in his eyes,
And hope in his heart as the daylight dies.
The Sun melts like snow in winters,
While shadows stretch like broken splinters.

The soul nurtures the existence, and what to question.
When a person sits by the sunset's shimmer,
A river of thoughts flows through the mind,
As if the fading night holds every light.

11. Veins of Gold: The Pulse of Humanity

Humanity blooms like a tender heart,
Soft beats flowing through veins of gold.
Empathy flows in quiet streams,
Binding strangers beneath the same sky.

A hand held, a tear wiped,
Warmth threading through silent walls.
Laughter rises like sunlight,
Breaking shadows where sorrow crawls.

Hearts throb beneath shared stars,
Mumbles of kindness shaping the dawn.
Unity hums in the pulse of the earth,
As humanity lifts unbroken, reborn.

12. The Unending Song of Pauses and Performance

*Some endings are beginnings, and some beginnings
become endings,
A bird soars dusk, yet sings at dawn.
Feathers torn mid-flight, yet winds keep mending,
A quiet song reborn when night is gone.*

**Wings stretch beneath a heavy, crimson sky,
Yet shadows bloom beneath a golden light.
A broken feather learns again to fly,
The heart still soaring through the fading night.**

*Endings hum beneath the beat of restless wings,
Yet morning paints the sky with quiet gold.
A single note reborn each time it sings,
Though skies grow dark, the flight remains unsaid.*

13. Journey to Hope

Hope and expectations are poles apart,
For those we trust can shatter the heart.
My heart sang lullabies of rainbows bright,
Yearning to spread wings in the darkened night.

Life may seem an endless, shadowed cave,
Yet seek the final ray, the light that saves.
In that glimmer, find strength anew,
Emerging from darkness, with a clearer view.

Enclasp the journey, both trials and grace,
For within the struggle, hope finds its place.

14. The Silent Tempest

A storm rages beneath quiet eyes,
Resounding of silent screams lost in the wind.
Expectations weigh heavy, a mirror of broken glass,
Shattered beneath the weight of reality.

Emotions drown beneath the surface,
Smiles stretched thin like fading light.
Thoughts spiral, crashing like restless waves,
Overthinking gnawing at fragile seams.

It kills in silence, a quiet implosion,
While the storm howls beneath a calm sky.

15. Shadows of an Unheard Cry

Loneliness is a restaurant where anxiety is served
In the night time when darkness takes over
And silence spreads its silent wings

The existence of one lingers in question
To find an answer to the unknown mist
Heart cries the tears of the unsaid

Soul wanders through ripples of the thoughts unseen,
where one's whispers reverberate, cold and keen
Lost in the maze of memories in between.

Moonlight drizzles like silver sorrow,
painting hollow shadows on the happiness that was
borrowed,

Each breath lives on a rented floor
Knocking on doors that open no more..

Hope, pulses like a candle in the tempest,
Quivering beneath the weight of despair,
Yet even in the quiet ache of seclusion ,
longing hums its unanswered prayer.

16. The Fallen Metaphor

Wounded and tormented
My Soul Apart
Confidence and happiness
Shattered like glass
I wanted someone to listen to me
But had to seal everything in my heart

My eyes kept searching for hope
And I could see a shadow pulling me towards happiness
with a soulful rope
My world crashed with every pulsating moment
I swirled underneath my pillow to feel the rhythm of my
heart
But all I heard was the silence speaking,
The tale of the unsaid, quietly seeping.

Reflections of phantoms danced through the night,
Murmurs of my longing were lost in the pale twilight.

17. The Moony Bonds

Like stars glimmer in the darkest sky amid the silent
thunderstorm
Freiends shine like seven colours of rainbow piercing the
hailstorm
When one opens window to feel the air
Friends are like a pleasant air that kisses their cheeks
with happiness

They light up the soul with warmth and grace,
A steady hand in life's cruel race.
Through storms and calm, they always stay,
Guiding hearts when skies turn grey.

Through every fall, they lift us high,
A constant star in the midnight sky.

18. Petals on Ice

A heart that refuses to heal,
Turns cold, a stone beneath the storm.
Chaos floods through restless veins,
Yet no tide can stir its core.

The mind, a stage where shadows play,
Hides healing's touch, and holds it bay.
Love's fragile bonds, a painful sting,
Where frozen petals softly cling.

A silent hum, a heart's dark art,
Yearning for solace, set apart.

19. Two Sides of Me

I wear a mask,
smooth as porcelain,
smiling when it should,
silent when it must.
It fits too well sometimes,
like it was made for me
or maybe I was made for it.

Behind it, I hold a coin,
turning between my fingers.
Two sides,
heads and tails,
light and shadow,
truth and lie.

Some days I'm the face of the Sun,
warm, bright,
offering light to everyone I touch.
Other days,
I'm the shadow behind the moon,

cold and quiet,
waiting for the dark to pass.

The mask fools them all
the laughter convincing,
the kindness effortless.
But the coin weighs heavy in my palm,
reminding me
that balance is fragile,
and the line between light and dark
is thin enough to break.

Heads, I am strong.
Tails, I am lost.
Heads, I give.
Tails, I take.
I smile,
but behind the mask,
I wonder
which side is truly me?

20. To the Star That Never Left

The Moon became my muser,
and the moonlight, my galore of light.
Under the sky full of stars,
my eyes kept searching
for that one shooting star
that had fallen to the ground
a quiet reminder
that even light has its fall.

The night whispered secrets
I wasn't ready to hear.
Shadows curled at my feet,
soft as breath, heavy as silence.
The moonlight kissed my face,
cold and silver,
like a goodbye I didn't know I'd been given.

Death stood at the edge of my thoughts,
gentle and patient,

not a thief, but a quiet companion
waiting with folded hands,
as if it knew
that falling is not the end,
but the beginning of stillness.

My words scattered like stardust,
some lost to the night,
others lingering in the quiet of my soul.
And as I closed the last page,
the moon smiled faintly,
its light spilling onto the ground
like the remnants of a broken star.

Perhaps it was never about finding the light
but knowing that even in the dark,
I was never alone.